ESSENTIAL MADRID TR

2023

A Comprehensive Guide for exploring Madrid,
to the Best Museums, Parks, and Restaurants,
Culture, History, and Cuisine,
Must-See Sights and Must-Try Experiences,
and Insider Tips for a Memorable Trip"

C. HILLARY

TABLE OF CONTENTS

INTRODUCTION

BRIEF HISTORY AND BACKGROUND
INFORMATION OF MADRID

OVERVIEW OF MADRID'S MAIN
ATTRACTIONS AND UNIQUE
CHARACTERISTICS

GETTING TO MADRID

TIPS FOR GETTING AROUND THE CITY:
INFORMATION ON PUBLIC
TRANSPORTATION, TAXIS, AND RENTAL
CARS
INFORMATION ON BUDGET-FRIENDLY
OPTIONS, AS WELL AS LUXURY HOTELS
AND RESORTS
THINGS TO DO IN MADRID AS A
VISITOR

RECOMMENDATIONS FOR UNIQUE EXPERIENCE: FLAMENCO SHOW, A FOOD TOUR, OR A DAY TRIP TO NEARBY TOLEDO FOR VISITORS IN MADRID

DINING IN MADRID

MADRID CULINARY GUIDE

NIGHTLIFE IN MADRID

NIGHTLIFE SAFETY TIPS

ESSENTIAL INFORMATION FOR TRAVELERS: INCLUDING VISA REQUIREMENTS, CURRENCY EXCHANGE, AND EMERGENCY CONTACTS

TIPS FOR STAYING SAFE AND HEALTHY DURING YOUR TRIP TO MADRID

MADRID DRESSING TIPS

INTRODUCTION

As I walked through the streets of Madrid, the hustle and bustle of the city filled my senses. The sights, sounds, and smells were overwhelming in the best possible way. I was excited to explore this vibrant city and immerse myself in the culture.

My first stop was the famous Prado Museum. As an art lover, I was eager to see the masterpieces housed within its walls. The sheer size of the museum was daunting, but I was determined to see as much as possible. From Goya's haunting "Black Paintings" to Velázquez's "Las Meninas," the collection did not disappoint.

After a few hours at the museum, I ventured out into the streets again. I stumbled upon a small tapas bar and decided to take a break and sample some of Madrid's famous cuisine. The plates of jamón ibérico, patatas bravas, and tortilla española were a revelation. I savored every bite, washing it down with a glass of crisp white wine.

As the sun began to set, I made my way to the iconic Puerta del Sol. The plaza was filled with people, all of whom seemed to be enjoying themselves. I watched as street performers entertained the crowds, while vendors sold everything from churros to souvenirs.

As darkness fell, I made my way to the rooftop terrace of my hotel. From here, I had a stunning view of the city lit up at night. The Royal Palace, with its grand façade and illuminated gardens, was particularly impressive. I lingered there for a while, soaking up the beauty of Madrid at night.

The next day, I explored the vibrant neighborhood of Malasaña, known for its street art and eclectic shops. I wandered through the narrow streets, admiring the colorful murals and unique storefronts. I even stumbled upon a vintage clothing store and found a one-of-a-kind dress that I knew would be the envy of my friends back home.

As my trip to Madrid came to an end, I realized that I had only scratched the surface of what this city had to offer. There were still museums to visit, neighborhoods to explore, and more tapas to try. I promised myself that I would return someday and experience all that Madrid had to offer once again.

Here are things to know about Madrid;

Madrid, the vibrant capital of Spain, is a city that truly has it all. From its rich history and culture to its lively nightlife and culinary scene, Madrid is a destination that offers something for every type of traveler.

Nestled in the heart of Spain, Madrid is a bustling metropolis that boasts a population of over 3 million people. Founded in the 9th century, the city has a rich history that is evident in its many historic landmarks, museums, and art galleries. The city has been shaped by its past, with influences from the Moors, the Habsburgs, and the Bourbons, making it a unique blend of cultures and traditions.

The city's most famous landmark is the Royal Palace of Madrid, which was once the official residence of the Spanish monarchs. The palace is a stunning example of 18th-century architecture, with over 3,000 rooms and a collection of priceless artwork and antiques. Visitors can tour the palace and its gardens to experience the opulence and grandeur of the Spanish royal family.

Another must-see attraction in Madrid is the Prado Museum, which houses one of the world's most extensive collections of European art. The museum features works by Spanish artists such as Velázquez, Goya, and El Greco, as well as international masters like Rembrandt and Rubens. The museum is a treasure trove of art and history, offering visitors a glimpse into the artistic and cultural heritage of Spain and Europe.

For those looking for a taste of Madrid's vibrant culture, there is no shortage of options. The city is known for its lively nightlife, with bars, clubs, and restaurants that cater to all tastes and preferences. Visitors can indulge in traditional Spanish tapas or sample international cuisine from around the world. Madrid is also home to a thriving arts and music scene, with numerous theaters and music venues that host performances by local and international artists.

One of the best ways to experience Madrid's vibrant culture is to attend a traditional Spanish bullfight. Although controversial, bullfighting is an important part of Spanish culture, and the spectacle is a must-see for many visitors. The bullfighting season runs from March to October, and tickets can be purchased in advance or at the gate.

Despite its bustling urban environment, Madrid is also home to many parks and green spaces. The Retiro Park is one of the city's most popular attractions, featuring beautiful gardens, lakes, and sculptures. Visitors can take a leisurely stroll or rent a rowboat to explore the park's many attractions.

In conclusion, Madrid is a city that has something for everyone. With its rich history, vibrant culture, and bustling urban environment, the city offers a unique and unforgettable travel experience. Whether you're interested in art and history, nightlife and entertainment, or simply soaking up the atmosphere of a bustling European metropolis, Madrid is the perfect destination for your next adventure.

BRIEF HISTORY AND BACKGROUND INFORMATION OF MADRID

Madrid, the capital of Spain, has a rich history and cultural heritage that dates back to prehistoric times. The first known settlement in the area was established by the Celts in the 2nd millennium BC, followed by the Romans in the 2nd century BC who named the city "Matrice".

In the 8th century, the city was conquered by the Moors and became a key strategic point in the region. However, in 1085, the city was reconquered by the Christians under the leadership of King Alfonso VI of Castile, who made it the capital of his kingdom.

Madrid continued to thrive under subsequent monarchs, particularly during the reign of the Habsburgs in the 16th and

17th centuries, when the city became a center of culture and commerce.

During the 18th century, Madrid underwent a major transformation under the reign of King Philip V, who commissioned the construction of many of the city's most iconic buildings, such as the Royal Palace of Madrid and the Plaza Mayor. This period also saw the establishment of many of the city's renowned cultural institutions, including the Royal Academy of Fine Arts and the Royal Botanic Garden.

In the 19th century, Madrid experienced a period of political instability and social unrest, marked by a series of uprisings and revolutions.

However, the city continued to grow and develop, particularly in the second half of the century, with the construction of new neighborhoods and the expansion of the city's infrastructure.

The 20th century brought significant changes to Madrid, particularly in the aftermath of the Spanish Civil War (1936-1939) and the subsequent dictatorship of General Francisco Franco.

During this time, Madrid became a center of opposition to the regime, with many intellectuals and artists expressing their dissent through their work.

Following Franco's death in 1975, Spain transitioned to a democracy, and Madrid emerged as a vibrant cultural and economic center.

The city hosted the 1982 FIFA World Cup, which brought international attention and investment to the city. In the decades since, Madrid has continued to grow and develop, with the construction of new buildings and infrastructure, including the impressive Barajas airport.

Today, Madrid is a bustling and cosmopolitan city, renowned for its rich history, culture, and art.

Visitors can explore the city's many museums, galleries, and historic landmarks, including the Prado Museum, the Reina Sofia Museum, and the Royal Palace.

Madrid is also known for its vibrant nightlife, with numerous bars, clubs, and restaurants offering a variety of entertainment options.

With its combination of historic charm and modern sophistication, Madrid continues to be one of Europe's most popular destinations.

OVERVIEW OF MADRID'S MAIN ATTRACTIONS AND UNIQUE CHARACTERISTICS

Madrid is the capital of Spain and is a vibrant city that offers visitors a unique blend of history, culture, and entertainment. Some of Madrid's main attractions and unique characteristics include:

Museums: Madrid is home to some of the best museums in the world, such as the Prado Museum, which houses a vast collection of Spanish and European art from the 12th to the 19th centuries. Other notable museums include the Reina Sofia Museum, which features contemporary art, and the

Thyssen-Bornemisza Museum, which has an extensive collection of European art.

Royal Palace: The Royal Palace of Madrid is a must-see attraction for visitors. It is the official residence of the Spanish Royal Family and has over 3,000 rooms, making it one of the largest palaces in Europe.

Plaza Mayor: This iconic square in the heart of Madrid has been a meeting point for locals and visitors for centuries. It is surrounded by stunning buildings and is a great place to watch, shop, and dine.

Food and Drink: Madrid is famous for its delicious cuisine, with dishes such as Cocido Madrileño, a hearty stew made with chickpeas and meat, and Churros con Chocolate, a sweet pastry served with thick hot chocolate. Visitors can also enjoy the local wine and beer.

Parks and Gardens: Madrid is a green city with many parks and gardens. The Retiro Park is the most famous, with over 125 hectares of green space, a lake, and a Crystal Palace. Other notable parks include the Casa de Campo and the Juan Carlos I Park.

Nightlife: Madrid has a vibrant nightlife, with many bars and clubs open until the early hours of the morning. The Malasaña neighborhood is popular with younger crowds, while the Chueca neighborhood is known for its LGBTQ+ scene.

Football: Football is a big part of Madrid's culture, with two of the world's biggest clubs, Real Madrid and Atlético Madrid, based in the city. Visitors can attend matches and tour the stadiums.

Overall, Madrid is a city with something for everyone, from art and culture to food, nightlife, and sports.

GETTING TO MADRID

If you are planning a trip to Madrid, there are several ways to get there, and each option has its advantages and disadvantages.

By Plane:

Madrid has one of the busiest airports in Europe, Adolfo Suárez Madrid-Barajas Airport (MAD). It is located 12 km from the city center, and it is well connected to the city by public transportation, such as the metro, bus, and taxi. Many airlines operate direct flights to Madrid from major cities around the world, making it easy to get to

Madrid from almost anywhere. If you are traveling from Europe, you may also consider using low-cost airlines, such as Ryanair, EasyJet, or Vueling, to save money on your ticket.

By Train

Spain has a modern and efficient high-speed train network, which connects Madrid with many other cities in the country, such as Barcelona, Seville, Valencia, and Malaga. The trains are operated by Renfe, the Spanish national railway company, and offer comfortable and fast travel. The main train station in Madrid is Atocha, located in the city center, and it is connected to the metro and bus network. If you are traveling from another European city, you may also consider taking a train to Paris or Lisbon and then connecting to Madrid by train.

By Bus

Spain has an extensive network of long-distance buses, operated by companies such as Alza and Avanza. Buses are a cheaper alternative to trains and planes, but they take longer to get to Madrid. Most buses arrive at the Estación Sur de Autobuses, located in the southern part of the city, which is also connected to the metro and bus network. If you are traveling from a nearby city, such as Toledo or Segovia, you may also consider taking a local bus or a regional train to Madrid.

By Car

Driving to Madrid can be a good option if you want to explore the countryside or visit other cities along the way. However, driving in Madrid can be challenging, as the city has a complex road network and heavy traffic. Parking in the city center can also be expensive and difficult to find. If you are driving from another city in Spain, such as Barcelona or Valencia, you can take the AP-7 or A-3 highways, respectively. If you are driving from Portugal or France, you can take the A-5 or A-6 highways, respectively.

In conclusion, there are several ways to get to Madrid, and each option has its pros and cons. Whether you choose to fly, take the train, bus, or drive, make sure to plan your trip in advance, book your tickets, and consider the time and cost involved. Madrid is a fantastic destination that offers a wealth of cultural and entertainment options, and getting there is just the first step of your journey.

TIPS FOR GETTING AROUND THE CITY: INFORMATION ON PUBLIC TRANSPORTATION, TAXIS, AND RENTAL CARS

Madrid is a beautiful city and there are many ways to get around it. Here are some tips to help visitors navigate the city.

Public Transportation

Madrid has an extensive public transportation system that is efficient and affordable. There are buses, metros, and trains that can take you almost anywhere in the city.

The Metro is the quickest and easiest way to get around Madrid. It has 12 lines and over 300 stations, so it is very easy to get from one place to another. The trains run from 6 am until 1:30 am on weekdays and until 2:30 am on weekends. A single ticket costs

€1.50, and you can also buy a 10-ride ticket () for €12.20.

Buses are also a good option for getting around Madrid. There are over 200 bus lines that run throughout the city. The buses run from 6 am until midnight, and a single ticket costs €1.50.

Taxis

Taxis are readily available in Madrid, and they are a convenient way to get around the city. They are also relatively affordable compared to other European cities. You can hail a taxi on the street or find one at a taxi stand. The fares are regulated by the city, and there are no additional charges for luggage or extra passengers. Taxis are also a good option for late-night travel when public transportation may not be available.

Rental Cars

If you prefer to drive yourself around the city, rental cars are available in Madrid. However, driving in the city can be challenging, especially for those who are not used to the traffic and narrow streets. Parking can also be difficult to find and expensive. If you do decide to rent a car, make sure to familiarize yourself with the city's driving laws and regulations.

Other Tips

Consider getting a Madrid Tourist Travel Pass (Abono Turístico) if you plan to use public transportation frequently. It allows for unlimited use of the Metro, buses, and trains for a set number of days.

If you are planning to visit museums and other attractions, consider purchasing a Madrid Card. It offers discounts on admission fees and includes free public transportation.

Use a map or GPS to navigate the city. Madrid can be confusing for first-time visitors, and it's easy to get lost.

Be aware of pickpockets, especially in crowded areas and on public transportation. Keep your belongings close and be vigilant.

Learn a few basic phrases in Spanish. While many people in Madrid speak English, it's always helpful to know a few key phrases.

Conclusion

Madrid is a beautiful city with many options for getting around. Public transportation is efficient and affordable, and taxis are readily available. Rental cars are an option for those who prefer to drive, but be aware of the challenges of driving in the city. With these tips, visitors can navigate Madrid with ease and enjoy all that the city has to offer.

MADRID ACCOMMODATION GUIDE

Madrid, the vibrant and bustling capital of Spain, offers a wide range of accommodation options for visitors. From luxury hotels to budget-friendly hostels, Madrid has something for everyone. In this article, we will provide a guide to help you choose where to stay in Madrid as a visitor.

Centro
The Centro district is the heart of Madrid and is home to many of the city's main attractions, including the Puerta del Sol, the Plaza Mayor, and the Royal Palace. The area is well-connected by public transport, making it easy to explore other parts of the city.

The Centro district is also known for its lively nightlife, with many bars and restaurants open until late. Accommodation options in Centro range from luxury hotels to budget-friendly hostels, so there is something to suit every budget.

Salamanca

The Salamanca district is one of Madrid's most upscale neighborhoods, known for its high-end shops, designer boutiques, and chic restaurants. The area is popular with affluent locals and visitors who are looking for a luxurious experience. The Salamanca district is well-connected by public transport, with several metro stations in the area. Accommodation options in Salamanca tend to be on the higher end of the price range, with many four- and five-star hotels and luxury apartments.

Chueca

The Chueca district is one of Madrid's most vibrant and colorful neighborhoods, known for its LGBT-friendly atmosphere, trendy bars, and lively nightlife. The area is popular with young people and visitors who are looking for a fun and lively atmosphere. Chueca is also home to several cultural attractions, including the Mercado de San Antón and the Museo del Romanticismo. Accommodation options in Chueca range from budget-friendly hostels to trendy boutique hotels.

Lavapiés

The Lavapiés district is one of Madrid's most diverse and multicultural neighborhoods, known for its bohemian atmosphere, colorful street art, and alternative music venues. The area is popular with young people and artists who are looking for a creative and inspiring environment. Lavapiés is also home to several cultural attractions, including the Teatro Valle-Inclán and the Casa Encendida. Accommodation options in Lavapiés tend to be more affordable than in other parts of the city, with many budget-friendly hostels and apartments.

Malasaña
The Malasaña district is one of Madrid's trendiest neighborhoods, known for its vintage shops, quirky boutiques, and independent galleries. The area is popular with hipsters and creatives who are looking for a unique and offbeat atmosphere. Malasaña is also home to several cultural attractions, including the Conde Duque Cultural Center and the San Antón Market. Accommodation options in Malasaña range from budget-friendly hostels to trendy boutique hotels.

Retiro

The Retiro district is one of Madrid's most picturesque neighborhoods, known for its beautiful parks, elegant architecture, and sophisticated restaurants. The area is popular with visitors who are looking for a more relaxed and upscale atmosphere. Retiro is also home to several cultural attractions, including the Prado Museum and the Reina Sofia Museum. Accommodation options in Retiro tend to be on the higher end of the price range, with many four- and five-star hotels and luxury apartments.

Sol:

Sol is the heart of Madrid and the most central neighborhood in the city. It's known for its bustling energy, with plenty of shops, restaurants, and entertainment options. Visitors will find the famous Plaza Mayor, the Puerta del Sol, and the Gran Vía shopping street all within walking distance.

Recommended accommodations in Sol include the Hotel Petit Palace Puerta del Sol and the Hotel Catalonia Puerta del Sol.

La Latina:
La Latina is an old and traditional neighborhood in the center of Madrid, known for its narrow streets, historic buildings, and lively atmosphere. It's a popular area for tapas bars and nightlife, and visitors can find the famous El Rastro flea market and the San Francisco el Grande basilica in this area. Recommended accommodations in La Latina include the Posada del León de Oro and the Hotel Puerta de Toledo.

Gran Vía
Gran Vía is one of the most famous streets in Madrid, known for its theaters, shopping, and nightlife.

It is a bustling area with plenty of restaurants, bars, and cafes. Accommodations in this area range from luxurious hotels to budget-friendly hostels. The Vincci Via 66 Hotel is a popular choice for its central location and modern amenities.

Barrio de las Letras

Barrio de las Letras, also known as the Literary Quarter, is a historic neighborhood known for its connections to famous writers and poets. It is a charming area with narrow streets, small squares, and traditional taverns. Accommodations in Barrio de las Letras range from budget-friendly hostels to elegant boutique hotels. The Hotel Villa Real is a luxurious hotel with a rooftop terrace, located in the heart of the neighborhood.

In conclusion, Madrid offers a diverse range of neighborhoods and accommodation options for visitors. Whether you are looking for a lively and colorful atmosphere or a more upscale and sophisticated environment, Madrid has something to offer. By choosing the right neighborhood, you can make the most of your visit to this vibrant and exciting city.

INFORMATION ON BUDGET-FRIENDLY OPTIONS, AS WELL AS LUXURY HOTELS AND RESORTS

Madrid, the capital of Spain, is a city that boasts of rich culture, exquisite architecture, and stunning museums. It is a city that offers something for everyone, from those on a budget to luxury travelers. There are several budget-friendly options as well as luxury hotels and resorts in Madrid to choose from.

Budget-Friendly Hotels and Hostels in Madrid

Ok Hostel Madrid
Ok Hostel Madrid is located in the heart of Madrid and is a budget-friendly option for

travelers. The hostel offers both dormitory-style rooms and private rooms. The rooms are clean, comfortable, and well-maintained. The hostel has a rooftop terrace that offers stunning views of the city. It is also located close to the Gran Via, which is one of the main shopping streets in Madrid.

Hostal Gala Madrid
Hostal Gala Madrid is located in the Malasaña neighborhood, which is known for its vibrant nightlife. The hostel offers clean and comfortable rooms at an affordable price. The rooms come with a private bathroom and air conditioning. The hostel is also located close to several restaurants and bars.

Room007 Chueca Hostel
Room007 Chueca Hostel is located in the Chueca neighborhood, which is known for its LGBTQ-friendly atmosphere. The hostel offers both private and shared rooms. The

rooms are clean and comfortable and come with a private bathroom. The hostel has a rooftop terrace that offers stunning views of the city.

Mad4You Hostel

Mad4You Hostel is located in the trendy Malasaña neighborhood. The hostel offers both private and shared rooms. The rooms are clean, comfortable, and well-maintained. The hostel has a rooftop terrace that offers stunning views of the city. It is also located close to several restaurants and bars.

Luxury Hotels and Resorts in Madrid

Gran Meliá Palacio de los Duques

Gran Meliá Palacio de los Duques is a luxury hotel located in the heart of Madrid. The hotel is housed in a 19th-century palace and offers stunning views of the Royal Palace. The rooms are luxurious and come with a private bathroom, air conditioning, and a flat-screen TV. The hotel has a spa, fitness center, and several restaurants.

Villa Magna Hotel

Villa Magna Hotel is a luxury hotel located in the exclusive Salamanca neighborhood. The hotel offers luxurious rooms that come with a private bathroom, air conditioning, and a flat-screen TV. The hotel has a spa, fitness center, and several restaurants. It is also located close to several high-end shops and restaurants.

Hotel Ritz Madrid

Hotel Ritz Madrid is a luxury hotel located in the heart of Madrid. The hotel is housed in a 1910 Belle Époque building and offers luxurious rooms that come with a private bathroom, air conditioning, and a flat-screen TV. The hotel has a spa, fitness center, and several restaurants. It is also located close to several museums and attractions.

The Principal Madrid Hotel
The Principal Madrid Hotel is a luxury hotel located in the Gran Via area of Madrid. The hotel offers luxurious rooms that come with a private bathroom, air conditioning, and a flat-screen TV. The hotel has a rooftop terrace that offers stunning views of the city. It is also located close to several restaurants and attractions.

In conclusion, Madrid offers a wide range of options for travelers, from budget-friendly hostels to luxurious hotels and resorts. It is a city that is sure to captivate and charm anyone who visits.

THINGS TO DO IN MADRID AS A VISITOR

Madrid, the capital of Spain, is a vibrant and exciting city with a rich history, stunning architecture, delicious food, and a lively nightlife. If you're visiting Madrid for the first time, there are plenty of things to see and do. In this guide, we'll highlight some of the best things to do in Madrid as a visitor.

Explore the Royal Palace of Madrid: The Royal Palace is one of the most iconic buildings in Madrid and a must-see attraction. The palace, which was built in the 18th century, is a stunning example of Baroque architecture and features over 3,000 rooms, including a throne room, banquet hall, and art gallery.

Visit the Prado Museum: The Prado Museum is one of the most important art museums in the world and a must-visit for art lovers. The museum houses an impressive collection of European art from the 12th to the 19th century, including works by Velázquez, Goya, and El Greco.

Wander around Retiro Park: Retiro Park is a beautiful oasis in the heart of Madrid and a great place to relax and unwind. The park features a large lake, rose garden, and various sculptures and monuments, including the famous Crystal Palace.

Explore the historic neighborhood of La Latina: La Latina is one of Madrid's oldest neighborhoods and is full of narrow streets, charming squares, and traditional bars and restaurants. It's a great place to wander around and soak up the atmosphere.

Try some tapas: Madrid is famous for its tapas, small plates of food that are perfect for sharing. Some of the best places to try tapas in Madrid include La Casa del Abuelo, El Sur, and El Tigre.

Watch a flamenco show: Flamenco is a traditional Spanish dance that originated in Andalusia, but you can find it all over Spain. Madrid has several flamenco venues, including Corral de la Morería, which is one of the oldest and most famous.

Take a day trip to Toledo: Toledo is a beautiful medieval city that's just a short train ride from Madrid. The city is full of historic landmarks, including the Alcázar of Toledo, Toledo Cathedral, and the Jewish Quarter.

Visit the Reina Sofia Museum: The Reina Sofia Museum is another important art museum in Madrid and is home to a collection of modern and contemporary art. The museum's most famous work is Picasso's Guernica, which is considered one of the most important paintings of the 20th century.

Watch a football match at Santiago Bernabéu Stadium: Madrid is home to two of the most successful football teams in the world, Real Madrid and Atlético Madrid. Watching a football match at Santiago Bernabéu Stadium is a great experience, even if you're not a fan of football.

Climb the Faro de Moncloa: The Faro de Moncloa is a 110-meter-high tower that offers panoramic views of the city. It's a great place to take photos and get a sense of the layout of Madrid.

In conclusion, Madrid is a city full of history, culture, and great food. Whether you're interested in art, architecture, or just soaking up the atmosphere, there's something for everyone in Madrid. Make sure to visit some of these top attractions to get the most out of your visit.

RECOMMENDATIONS FOR UNIQUE EXPERIENCE: FLAMENCO SHOW, A FOOD TOUR, OR A DAY TRIP TO NEARBY TOLEDO FOR VISITORS IN MADRID

Flamenco show at Corral de la Morería - This historic tablao in the heart of Madrid is considered one of the best places to see authentic flamenco. Enjoy a drink or dinner as you watch the passionate dancing, singing, and guitar playing.

Food tour of Madrid - Get a taste of the city's culinary delights on a food tour. Sample traditional tapas, fresh seafood, and sweets like churros and chocolate. Try a few of the local wines and learn about Madrid's food culture from an expert guide.

Day trip to Toledo - Just an hour's train ride from Madrid, this charming medieval town is a must-see for history buffs and architecture lovers. Explore the winding streets, admire the Gothic cathedral, and visit the famous El Greco Museum.

Hot air balloon ride - For a truly unique view of the city and surrounding countryside, take a hot air balloon ride.

Watch the sunrise or sunset as you soar over landmarks like the Royal Palace, Retiro Park, and the Sierra de Guadarrama mountain range.

Flamenco dance lesson - If you're feeling inspired after seeing a flamenco show, why not try a dance lesson? Learn the basic steps, rhythms, and hand movements from a professional dancer, and feel the passion and energy of this art form for yourself.

MADRID SHOPPING RECOMMENDATIONS

Madrid is a vibrant city with a diverse and exciting shopping scene. Whether you're looking for high-end designer boutiques, quirky independent stores, or traditional markets, Madrid has something to offer for everyone. Here is an overview of Madrid's shopping scene, including recommendations for markets, boutiques, and souvenir shops.

Markets:

El Rastro: Madrid's most famous open-air market, held every Sunday in the La Latina neighborhood. Here, you can find a wide range of goods, including antiques, clothing, accessories, and souvenirs. Be prepared to bargain!

Mercado San Miguel: This indoor market near Plaza Mayor is the perfect place to sample traditional Spanish cuisine, including tapas, wine, and gourmet products. It's a bit pricey, but definitely worth a visit.

Mercado de San Antón: This market in the Chueca neighborhood offers a more modern and upscale shopping experience, with gourmet food, fashion boutiques, and a rooftop terrace with stunning views of the city.

Boutiques:

Malababa: This Spanish brand offers stylish and affordable handbags, shoes, and accessories. Their flagship store in the trendy Malasaña neighborhood is a must-visit.

Paula Alonso: For high-end Spanish fashion, head to this boutique in the Salamanca neighborhood. They carry brands like Loewe, Balenciaga, and Isabel Marant.

El Ganso: This Madrid-based brand offers preppy, retro-inspired clothing for men and

women. Their flagship store on Calle Fuencarral is a colorful and quirky space that's worth a visit.
Souvenir Shops:

Casa de Diego: This iconic shop near Plaza Mayor has been selling traditional Spanish fans, umbrellas, and mantillas since 1858. It's the perfect place to pick up a unique and authentic souvenir.

La Favorita: For artisanal ceramics, head to this charming shop in the La Latina neighborhood. They offer a wide range of plates, bowls, and vases decorated with traditional Spanish motifs.

Chocolatería San Ginés: This historic café near the Puerta del Sol is famous for its churros and hot chocolate. It's the perfect place to grab a sweet treat and a souvenir tin of their delicious hot chocolate mix.

Gran Via: This is Madrid's most famous shopping street, where you can find everything from high-end fashion boutiques to chain stores.

Salamanca District: This upscale neighborhood is known for its designer boutiques and luxury brands.

DINING IN MADRID

Madrid is a vibrant city with plenty of dining options. Here are some suggestions for places to check out:

Botin: This historic restaurant has been around since 1725 and is known for its roasted suckling pig and lamb.

Sobrino de Botin: Another iconic restaurant that has been serving traditional Spanish dishes since 1892, including cocido (a hearty stew) and roast beef.

Casa Mono: This trendy restaurant serves contemporary Spanish cuisine, including tapas and creative small plates.

La Vaca y La Huerta: This farm-to-table restaurant focuses on organic, locally sourced ingredients and offers a rotating menu of seasonal dishes.
No matter where you go in Madrid, you're sure to find plenty of great shopping and dining options. Be sure to explore the city's many neighborhoods and try some of the local specialties.

MADRID CULINARY GUIDE

Madrid is a city with a rich and diverse culinary scene, offering a variety of traditional Spanish dishes as well as trendy restaurants serving contemporary cuisine. Here's a guide to some of the best places to eat in Madrid:

Traditional Spanish dishes:

Cocido Madrileño: This hearty stew is a staple of Madrid cuisine, made with chickpeas, vegetables, and various meats like chorizo and beef.

Huevos Rotos: This simple but delicious dish consists of fried eggs served over a bed of fried potatoes, often topped with slices of cured ham or chorizo.

Callos a la Madrileña: This is a tripe stew that includes chickpeas, chorizo, and morcilla (Spanish black pudding).

Churros con Chocolate: This classic Spanish dessert consists of fried dough served with a thick, hot chocolate dipping sauce.

Tortilla de Patatas: A thick omelet made with potatoes and onions, often served as a tapa.

Trendy Restaurants:

DiverXO: This three-Michelin-starred restaurant is a must-visit for foodies. Chef David Muñoz's avant-garde cuisine pushes the boundaries of traditional Spanish cooking.

StreetXO: Also run by Chef David Muñoz, StreetXO offers a more casual dining experience, serving Asian-inspired street food with a Spanish twist.

Ramen Kagura: This popular ramen joint serves up delicious bowls of Japanese-style noodles with a variety of toppings.

Punto MX: This upscale Mexican restaurant offers a modern take on traditional Mexican cuisine, with dishes like tacos de chapulines (tacos with grasshoppers).

La Vaca y La Huerta: This farm-to-table restaurant focuses on local, organic ingredients and serves up tasty, creative dishes like roast beef with parsnip puree and carrot chips.

Other Recommendations:

Mercado de San Miguel: This historic market is a foodie paradise, with over 30 stalls serving up a variety of Spanish specialties like Iberico ham, seafood, and paella.

Casa Botín: Established in 1725, Casa Botín is the oldest restaurant in the world according to Guinness World Records. It's famous for its succulent roast suckling pig and roast lamb.

La Casa del Abuelo: This traditional tapas bar is a Madrid institution, known for its signature dish of grilled prawns.

La Taberna de la Daniela: A cozy, family-run restaurant that serves up delicious, homemade Spanish dishes like croquettes and patatas bravas.

El Corte Inglés Gourmet Experience: Located on the top floor of a department store, this food hall offers a variety of gourmet food stalls and restaurants, with stunning views of the city.

NIGHTLIFE IN MADRID

Madrid is well known for its vibrant nightlife, which offers a wide variety of options for party-goers of all tastes and ages. From traditional tapas bars to upscale nightclubs and live music venues, the city has something for everyone.

Bars:

One of the best ways to experience Madrid's nightlife is by visiting its many bars. The city is famous for its traditional tapas bars, where locals enjoy a glass of wine or beer accompanied by small plates of delicious snacks. Some of the most popular tapas bars in Madrid include El Tigre, Casa Alberto, and Bodegas Ricla.

For a more upscale experience, visitors can head to cocktail bars like Salmon Guru, a speakeasy-style bar located in the trendy Malasaña neighborhood, or the stylish rooftop terrace of the Círculo de Bellas Artes cultural center.

Clubs:

Madrid is home to some of the best nightclubs in Europe, with a thriving electronic music scene that attracts top DJs from around the world. One of the most famous clubs in Madrid is Joy Eslava, a historic venue that has been hosting parties since the 1980s. Other popular clubs include Fabrik, an enormous warehouse-style club located just outside the city center, and Kapital, a multi-level club that features different music genres on each floor.

Live music venues:
Madrid has a vibrant live music scene, with many venues that showcase local and international acts. For jazz lovers, the Café Central is a must-visit, with nightly performances by some of the best jazz musicians in the world. Another popular venue is the Teatro Barceló, a historic theater that has been converted into a nightclub with live music performances. The Sala Mon Live is also a great option, hosting concerts by both established and up-and-coming artists.

Overall, Madrid's nightlife scene is diverse and exciting, with something for everyone. Visitors should be sure to explore different neighborhoods and venues to get the most out of their experience.

NIGHTLIFE SAFETY TIPS

Madrid is known for its vibrant nightlife, with many bars, clubs, and restaurants open late into the night. Here are some tips for staying safe while enjoying Madrid's nightlife:

Stick to well-lit and busy areas: Avoid walking in dark and isolated streets or alleys, especially at night. Stick to well-lit and busy areas, and consider taking a taxi or public transportation to get around.

Keep an eye on your belongings: Madrid is known for pickpocketing, so make sure you keep an eye on your belongings, especially in crowded areas such as bars and clubs. Keep your valuables close to you, preferably in a bag or a pocket with a zipper.

Drink responsibly: Excessive alcohol consumption can make you more vulnerable to theft, assault, and accidents. Pace yourself and know your limits, and consider drinking water or non-alcoholic beverages in between drinks.

Use official taxis: If you need to take a taxi, use official taxis, which are typically white with a red stripe and have a light on the roof. Avoid unmarked taxis, as they can be unsafe and may overcharge you.

Stay with friends: It's always safer to go out with a group of friends, and to stick together throughout the night. If someone needs to leave early, make sure they have a safe way to get home.

Be aware of your surroundings: Stay alert and aware of your surroundings, and trust your instincts. If something feels wrong or unsafe, leave the area or ask for help.

Plan your route ahead of time: Before heading out, plan your route and make sure you know how to get back to your accommodation safely. If you're not sure, ask for advice from your hotel or a trusted local.

ESSENTIAL INFORMATION FOR TRAVELERS: INCLUDING VISA REQUIREMENTS, CURRENCY EXCHANGE, AND EMERGENCY CONTACTS

Here is some essential information for travelers:

1.Visa Requirements:
Before traveling, it is essential to check the visa requirements for the destination you are traveling to. Some countries offer visa-free entry for a certain period, while others require a visa for entry. Make sure to check the visa requirements well in advance to avoid any last-minute complications.

2. Currency Exchange:
When traveling internationally, you will need to exchange your home currency for the local currency of the country you are visiting. You can exchange currency at airports, banks, or currency exchange

offices. It's important to research the exchange rate and compare rates to get the best deal.

3. Emergency Contacts:
It is always good to have emergency contacts with you while traveling. Make sure to write down important phone numbers like your embassy, local emergency services, and your hotel or accommodation.

4. Health Precautions:
It is essential to take care of your health while traveling. Research the required vaccinations, check the weather forecast, and pack accordingly. If you have any medical conditions, make sure to carry your medications with you.

5. Travel Insurance:
Travel insurance can protect you from unforeseen events like medical emergencies, trip cancellations, and theft. Make sure to

purchase travel insurance before you leave for your trip.

6. Language:
If you are traveling to a country where you don't speak the language, it is a good idea to learn some basic phrases or carry a translation app. It will help you navigate and communicate better.

7. Culture and Customs:
It's important to be aware of the culture and customs of the country you are visiting. Respect the local culture and follow their customs to avoid any misunderstandings or offense.

These are some essential information for travelers. Make sure to do your research and plan your trip accordingly to have a safe and enjoyable experience.

TIPS FOR STAYING SAFE AND HEALTHY DURING YOUR TRIP TO MADRID

Here are some tips for staying safe and healthy during your trip to Madrid:

Stay hydrated: Madrid can get very hot during the summer months, so it's important to drink plenty of water to stay hydrated. Carry a water bottle with you and refill it at the many public fountains located throughout the city.

Watch your belongings: Like any major city, Madrid has its share of pickpockets and petty crime. Be aware of your surroundings, keep your valuables close to you, and avoid carrying large amounts of cash.

Use sunscreen: The Spanish sun can be intense, even in the cooler months. Protect your skin by wearing sunscreen and a hat when you're out and about.

Eat well: Madrid is famous for its cuisine, but it's easy to overindulge in rich food and alcohol. Try to balance your meals with plenty of fruits, vegetables, and whole grains, and drink plenty of water.

Use public transportation: Madrid's public transportation system is safe, affordable, and efficient. Use the Metro or bus system to get around the city, and avoid taking unlicensed taxis.

Be respectful: Spanish culture places a high value on courtesy and politeness. Be respectful of the locals, their customs, and their language.

Learn some basic Spanish: While many people in Madrid speak English, it's always helpful to know some basic Spanish phrases. It will not only help you communicate better but also show your respect for the local culture.

Take care of your feet: Madrid is a walkable city, but all that walking can be hard on your feet. Wear comfortable shoes, take breaks when you need to, and consider getting a foot massage or reflexology treatment to help you relax.

Stay connected: Keep your family and friends informed of your whereabouts and any changes to your itinerary. Use a reliable phone or internet service to stay connected.

Get travel insurance: It's always a good idea to have travel insurance when you're visiting a foreign country. It can protect you in case of illness, injury, or other unexpected events.

MADRID DRESSING TIPS

Madrid is a city with a vibrant and lively culture, and visitors are encouraged to dress appropriately for the weather and the occasion. Here are some tips for dressing in Madrid:

Dress according to the season: Madrid can be quite hot in the summer months, so it's important to wear light and airy clothing. In the winter, the city can get quite cold, so it's a good idea to bring warm clothes such as coats, scarves, and hats.

Dress modestly: While Madrid is a cosmopolitan city, it is still important to dress modestly when visiting churches or other religious sites. Avoid wearing shorts, tank tops, or revealing clothing in these areas.

Comfortable footwear: Madrid is a city that is best explored on foot, so it's important to wear comfortable shoes. Avoid wearing high heels or shoes that are not suitable for walking long distances.

Dress for the occasion: Madrid has a diverse range of attractions, from museums and galleries to nightclubs and bars. Dress appropriately for the occasion, whether it's casual wear for sightseeing or more formal attire for a night out.

Consider the local style: Madrid has a distinct style that combines classic elegance with modern flair. Consider incorporating this style into your wardrobe by wearing classic pieces with a modern twist.

Overall, the key to dressing in Madrid is to be comfortable and respectful of the local culture. With the right attire, you can enjoy all that the city has to offer while looking stylish and appropriate.

Printed in Great Britain
by Amazon